ARKANSAS NURSE PRACTICE ACT

2009-2010 Edition

Law Offices of Lisa Douglas, PLLC
2300 Main Street
North Little Rock, AR 72114
(501) 798-0004
www.LisaGDouglas.com
LisaGDouglas@aol.com

TABLE OF CONTENTS

Professions, Occupations and Businesses, Title 17

Subchapter 7. Medication Assistive Persons

-----------------------------*Law Offices of Lisa Douglas, PLLC*-----------------------------

PROFESSIONS, OCCUPATIONS, AND BUSINESSES, Title 17
SUBTITLE 3. MEDICAL PROFESSIONS

§ 17-87-101. License Required-Purpose.

(a) In order to safeguard life and health, any person practicing or offering to practice nursing for compensation shall be required to submit evidence that he or she is qualified to so practice and shall be licensed as provided in this chapter:

(1) Professional nursing;

(2) Advanced practice nursing;

(3) Registered practitioner nursing;

(4) Practical nursing; or

(5) Psychiatric technician nursing.

(b) It shall be unlawful for any person not licensed by the board:

(1) To practice or offer to practice professional nursing, advanced practice nursing, registered practitioner nursing, practical nursing, or psychiatric technician nursing; or

(2) To use any sign, card, or device to indicate that the person is a professional registered nurse, an advanced practice nurse, a registered nurse practitioner, a licensed practical nurse, or a licensed psychiatric technician nurse.

History:

Acts 1971, No. 432, § 1; 1979, No. 613, § 1; 1980 (1st Ex. Sess.), No. 14, § 1; A.S.A. 1947, § 72-745; 1995, No. 409, § 1.

§ 17-87-102. Definitions

As used in this chapter:

(1) "Board" means the Arkansas State Board of Nursing;

(2) "Collaborative practice agreement" means a written plan that identifies a physician who agrees to collaborate with an advanced practice nurse in the joint management of the health care of the advanced practice nurse's patients, and outlines procedures for consultation with or referral to the collaborating physician or other health care professionals as indicated by a patient's health care needs;

(3) "Consulting physician" means a physician licensed under the Arkansas Medical Practices Act, §§ 17-95-201 — 17-95-207, 17-95-301 — 17-95-305, and 17-95-401 — 17-95-411, with obstetrical privileges in a hospital, who has agreed to practice in consultation with a certified nurse midwife; and

(4) (A) "Practice of advanced practice nursing" means the delivery of health care services for compensation by professional nurses who have gained additional knowledge and skills through successful completion of an organized program of nursing education that certifies nurses for advanced practice roles as advanced nurse practitioners, certified nurse anesthetists, certified nurse midwives, and clinical nurse specialists.

(B) (I) "Practice of advanced nurse practitioner nursing" means the performance for compensation of nursing skills by a registered nurse who, as demonstrated by national certification, has advanced knowledge and practice skills in the delivery of nursing services.

(ii) "Practice of certified registered nurse anesthesia" means the performance for compensation of advanced nursing skills relevant to the administration of anesthetics under the supervision of, but not necessarily in the presence of, a licensed physician, licensed dentist, or other person lawfully entitled to order anesthesia. A certified registered nurse anesthetist may order nurses, within their scope of practice, to administer drugs preoperatively and postoperatively in connection with an anesthetic or other operative or invasive procedure, or both, that will be or has been provided.

(iii) "Practice of clinical nurse specialist nursing" means the performance for compensation of nursing skills by a registered nurse who, through study and supervised practice at the graduate level and as evidenced by national certification, has advanced knowledge and practice skills in a specialized area of nursing practice;

(iv) "Practice of nurse midwifery" means the performance for compensation of nursing skills relevant to the management of women's health care, focusing on pregnancy, childbirth, the postpartum period, care of the newborn, family planning, and gynecological needs of women, within a health care system that provides for consultation, collaborative management, or referral as indicated by the health status of the client.

(5) "Practice of practical nursing" means the performance for compensation of acts involving the care of the ill, injured, or infirm or the delegation of certain nursing practices to other personnel as set forth in regulations established by the board under the direction of a registered professional nurse, an advanced practice nurse, a licensed physician, or a licensed dentist, which acts do not require the substantial specialized skill, judgment, and knowledge required in professional nursing;

(6) "Practice of professional nursing" means the performance for compensation of any acts involving:

(A) The observation, care, and counsel of the ill, injured, or infirm;

(B) The maintenance of health or prevention of illness of others;

(C) The supervision and teaching of other personnel;

(D) The delegation of certain nursing practices to other personnel as set forth in regulations established by the board; or

(E) The administration of medications and treatments as prescribed by practitioners authorized to prescribe and treat in accordance with state law where such acts require substantial specialized judgment and skill based on knowledge and application of the principles of biological, physical, and social sciences;

(7) "Practice of psychiatric technician nursing" means the performance for compensation of acts involving the care of the physically and mentally ill, retarded, injured, or infirm or the delegation of certain nursing practices to other personnel as set forth in regulations established by the board, and the carrying out of medical orders under the direction of a registered professional nurse, an advanced practice nurse, a licensed physician, or a licensed dentist, where such activities do not require the substantial specialized skill, judgment, and knowledge required in professional nursing; and

(8) (A) "Practice of registered nurse practitioner nursing" means the delivery of health care services for compensation in collaboration with and under the direction of a licensed physician or under the direction of protocols developed with a licensed physician.

(B) Registered nurse practitioners shall be authorized to engage in activities as

7

recognized by the nursing profession and as authorized by the board.

(C) Nothing in this subdivision (8) is to be deemed to limit a registered nurse practitioner from engaging in those activities which normally constitute the practice of nursing, or those which may be performed by persons without the necessity of the license to practice medicine.

History:

Acts 1971, No. 432, § 2; 1979, No. 404, §§ 1, 7; 1979, No. 613, § 2; A.S.A. 1947, § 72-746; Acts 1995, No. 409, § 2; 1997, No. 1065, § 1; 1999, No. 1208, § 1.

§ 17-87-103. Exceptions

This chapter does not prohibit:

(1) The furnishing of nursing assistance in an emergency;

(2) The practice of nursing that is incidental to their program of study by students enrolled in nursing education programs approved by the board;

(3) The practice of any legally qualified nurse of another state who is employed by the United States Government or any bureau, division, or agency while in the discharge of his or her official duties in installations where jurisdiction has been ceded by the State of Arkansas;

(4) The practice of any legally qualified and licensed nurse of another state, territory, or foreign country whose responsibilities include transporting patients into, out of, or through this state while actively engaged in patient transport that does not exceed forty-eight (48) hours in this state;

(5) Nursing or care of the sick when done in connection with the practice of the religious tenets of any church by its adherents;

(6) The care of the sick when done in accordance with the practice of religious principles or tenets of any well-recognized church or denomination that relies upon prayer or spiritual means of healing;

(7) The administration of anesthetics under the supervision of, but not necessarily in the presence of, a licensed physician, dentist, or other person lawfully entitled to order

8

anesthesia by a graduate nurse anesthetist awaiting certification results while holding a temporary permit;

(8) The administration of anesthetics under the supervision of, but not necessarily in the presence of, a licensed physician, dentist, or other person lawfully entitled to order anesthesia by a registered nurse who is enrolled as a bona fide student pursuing a course in a nurse anesthesia school that is approved by a nationally recognized accrediting body and whose graduates are acceptable for certification by a nationally recognized certifying body, provided the giving or administering of the anesthetics is confined to the educational requirements of the course and under the direct supervision of a qualified instructor;

(9) Hospital-employed professional paramedics from administering medication for diagnostic procedures under the direction of a physician;

(10) The prescription and administration of drugs, medicines, or therapeutic devices in the presence of and under the supervision of an advanced practice nurse holding a certificate of prescriptive authority, a licensed physician, or licensed dentist by a registered nurse who is enrolled as a student in an advanced pharmacology course, provided the prescription or administration of drugs or medicines, or both, is confined to the educational requirements of the course and under the direct supervision of a qualified instructor; or

(11) (A) Health maintenance activities by a designated care aide for a:

(I) Competent adult at the direction of the adult; or

(ii) Minor child or incompetent adult at the direction of a caretaker.

(B) As used in this section:

(I) "Caretaker" means a person who is:

(a) Directly and personally involved in providing care for a minor child or incompetent adult; and

(b) The parent, foster parent, family member, friend, or legal guardian of the minor child or incompetent adult receiving care under subdivision (11)(B)(i)(*a*) of this section;

(ii) "Competent adult" means an individual who:

(a) Is eighteen (18) years of age or older; and

(b) Has the capability and capacity to make an informed decision; and

(iii) "Health maintenance activities" means activities that:

(*a*) Enable a minor child or adult to live in his or her home; and

(*b*) Are beyond activities of daily living that:

(*1*) The minor child or adult is unable to perform for himself or herself; and

(*2*) The attending physician, advanced practice nurse, or registered nurse determines can be safely performed in the minor child's or adult's home by a designated care aide under the direction of a competent adult or caretaker.

(C) As used in this section, "home" does not include:

(i) A nursing home;

(ii) An assisted living facility;

(iii) A residential care facility;

(iv) An intermediate care facility; or

(v) A hospice care facility.

(D) The Arkansas State Board of Nursing with the input of the Home Health Care Service Agency Advisory Council, the Arkansas Health Care Association, and the Arkansas Residential Assisted Living Association shall promulgate rules specifying which health maintenance activities are not exempted under this subdivision (11) and the minimal qualifications required of the designated care aide.

History:

Acts 1971, No. 432, §§ 1, 2, 17; 1979, No. 404, §§ 1, 7; 1979, No. 613, §§ 1, 2; 1980 (1st Ex. Sess.), No. 14, §§ 1, 3; 1985, No. 189, § 2; A.S.A. 1947, §§ 72-745, 72-746, 72-761; Acts 1995, No. 409, § 3; 1997, No. 1065, § 2; 2005, No. 1440, § 1.

§ 17-87-104. Penalty

(a) (1) It shall be a misdemeanor for any person to:

(A) Sell or fraudulently obtain or furnish any nursing diploma, license, renewal, or record, or aid or abet therein;

(B) Practice nursing as defined by this chapter under cover of any diploma, license, or record illegally or fraudulently obtained or signed or issued unlawfully or under fraudulent representation;

(C) Practice professional nursing, advanced practice nursing, registered nurse practitioner nursing, practical nursing, or psychiatric technician nursing as defined by this chapter unless licensed by the Arkansas State Board of Nursing to do so;

(D) Use in connection with his or her name any of the following titles, names, or initials, if the user is not properly licensed under this chapter:

(i) Nurse;

(ii) Registered nurse or R.N.;

(iii) Advanced practice nurse or A.P.N., or any of the following:

(a) Advanced registered nurse practitioner, A.R.N.P., or A.N.P.;

(b) Nurse anesthetist, certified nurse anesthetist, certified registered nurse anesthetist, or C.R.N.A.;

(c) Nurse midwife, certified nurse midwife, licensed nurse midwife, C.N.M., or L.N.M.; or

(d) Clinical nurse specialist or C.N.S.;

(iv) Registered nurse practitioner, N.P., or R.N.P.;

(v) Licensed practical nurse, practical nurse, or L.P.N.;

(vi) Licensed psychiatric technician nurse, psychiatric technician nurse, L.P.T.N., or P.T.N.; or

(vii) Any other name, title, or initials that would cause a reasonable person to believe the user is licensed under this chapter;

(E) Practice professional nursing, advanced practice nursing, registered nurse practitioner nursing, practical nursing, or psychiatric technician nursing during the time his or her license shall be suspended;

(F) Conduct a nursing education program for the preparation of professional nurses, advanced practice nurses, nurse practitioners, practical nurses, or psychiatric technician nurses unless the program has been approved by the board;

(G) Prescribe any drug or medicine as authorized by this chapter unless certified by the board as having prescriptive authority, except that a certified registered nurse anesthetist shall not be required to have prescriptive authority to provide anesthesia care, including the administration of drugs or medicines necessary for the care; or

(H) Otherwise violate any provisions of this chapter.

(2) Such misdemeanor shall be punishable by a fine of not less than twenty-five dollars ($25.00) nor more than five hundred dollars ($500). Each subsequent offense shall be punishable by fine or by imprisonment of not more than thirty (30) days, or by both fine and imprisonment.

(b) (1) After providing notice and a hearing, the board may levy civil penalties in an amount not to exceed one thousand dollars ($1000) for each violation against those individuals or entities found to be in violation of this chapter or regulations promulgated thereunder.

(2) Each day of violation shall be a separate offense.

(3) These penalties shall be in addition to other penalties which may be imposed by the board pursuant to this chapter.

(4) Unless the penalty assessed under this subsection is paid within fifteen (15) calendar days following the date for an appeal from the order, the board shall have the power to file suit in the Circuit Court of Pulaski County to obtain a judgment for the amount of penalty not paid.

History:

Acts 1971, No. 432, § 18; Acts 1980 (1st Ex. Sess.), No. 14, § 4; A.S.A. 1947, § 72-762; Acts 1995, No. 409, § 4.

§ 17-87-105. Injunction

(a) The Circuit Court of Pulaski County is vested with jurisdiction and power to enjoin the unlawful practice of nursing in any county of the State of Arkansas in a proceeding by the board or by any member thereof or by any citizen in this state.

(b) The issuance of any injunction shall not relieve a person from criminal prosecution for violation of the provisions of this chapter. The remedy of injunction is to be in addition to liability for criminal prosecution.

History:

Acts 1971, No. 432, § 19; A.S.A. 1947, § 72-763.

§ 17-87-106. Construction of Chapter

Nothing in this chapter relating to the practice of advanced practice nursing shall be construed to limit or alter the scope of practice of any registered nurse practitioner or any other licensed nurse.

History:

Acts 1995, No. 409, § 21.

SUBCHAPTER 2-ARKANSAS STATE BOARD OF NURSING

§ 17-87-201. Creation-Members

(a) There is created the Arkansas State Board of Nursing, to be composed of thirteen (13) members to be appointed by the Governor for terms of four (4) years, subject to confirmation by the Senate.

(b) (1) Six (6) members shall be registered nurses whose highest level of educational preparation shall be as follows:

(A) Two (2) diploma-school graduates;

(B) Two (2) associate degree graduates; and

(C) Two (2) baccalaureate degree or postbaccalaureate degree graduates.

(2) Each registered nurse member of the board shall have the following qualifications:

(A) Be an Arkansas resident;

(B) Have at least five (5) years of successful experience as a registered nurse in nursing practice, administration, or teaching;

(C) Be licensed in Arkansas as a registered nurse; and

(D) Have been employed as a registered nurse for at least three (3) years immediately preceding appointment, two (2) of which shall have been in Arkansas.

(c) (1) One (1) member shall be a licensed advanced practice nurse.

(2) The licensed advanced practice nurse board member shall have the following qualifications:

(A) Be an Arkansas resident;

(B) Have at least five (5) years of experience as an advanced practice nurse;

(C) Be licensed in Arkansas as an advanced practice nurse;

(D) Have been actively engaged in nursing for at least three (3) years immediately preceding appointment, two (2) of which shall have been in Arkansas; and

(E) Have a certificate granting prescriptive authority.

(d) (1) Four (4) members shall be licensed practical nurses or licensed psychiatric technician nurses.

(2) Each licensed practical nurse board member or licensed psychiatric technician nurse board member shall have the following qualifications:

(A) Be an Arkansas resident;

(B) Have at least five (5) years of successful experience as a practical nurse or psychiatric technician nurse or as a teacher in an educational program to prepare practitioners of nursing;

(C) Be licensed in Arkansas as a licensed practical nurse or licensed psychiatric technician nurse; and

(D) Have been employed as a licensed practical nurse or as a licensed psychiatric technician nurse for at least three (3) years immediately preceding appointment, two (2) of which shall have been in Arkansas.

(e) One (1) member shall be a lay person representing consumers of health care services.

(f) One (1) member of the board shall not be actively engaged in or retired from the profession of nursing, shall be sixty (60) years of age or older, and shall be the representative of the elderly. This member shall be appointed from the state at large, subject to confirmation by the Senate, and shall be a full voting member but shall not participate in the grading of examinations.

(g) The consumer representative and the representative of the elderly positions may not be filled by the same person.

(h) No member shall be appointed to more than two (2) consecutive terms.

(i) Board members may receive expense reimbursement and stipends in accordance with § 25-16-901 et seq.

(j) The terms of all registered nurse members and advanced practice nurse members shall be four (4) years.

History:

Acts 1971, No. 432, §§ 3, 4; 1977, No. 113, §§ 1-3; 1979, No. 404, §§ 2, 3; 1981, No. 717, § 2; 1983, No. 131, §§ 1-3, 5; 1983, No. 135, §§ 1-3, 5; 1985, No. 189, § 1; A.S.A. 1947, §§ 6-617 — 6-619, 6-623 — 6-626, 72-747, 72-748; Acts 1995, No. 409, § 5; 1997, No. 250, § 159; 1999, No. 941, § 1; 2001, No. 149, §§ 1, 2; 2007, No. 205, § 1.

§ 17-87-202. Organization and Proceedings

(a) (1) It shall be the duty of the Arkansas State Board of Nursing to meet regularly at least one (1) time every six (6) months for the purpose of conducting its business.

(2) Special meetings of the board may be called at any time at the pleasure of the President of the Arkansas State Board of Nursing or by the Secretary of the Arkansas State Board of Nursing on the request of any three (3) members of the board.

(3) A majority of the members shall constitute a quorum at any meeting of the board.

(4) The board shall determine by its own rules the time and manner of giving notice of meetings to its members.

(5) The giving of an examination for licensure shall not be considered as a meeting of the board.

(b) The secretary shall keep a record of the minutes of the meetings of the board, together with a record of the action of the board thereon. The records shall at all reasonable times be open for public inspection.

(c) The board shall maintain an office for the administration of its business. The board shall annually elect a president, vice president, secretary, and treasurer from among its members. The president of the board shall be a registered nurse.

(d) The executive director of the board shall be a registered nurse and meet the qualifications required by the board.

History:

Acts 1971, No. 432, §§ 4, 8, 9; 1979, No. 404, §§ 3, 5, 6; A.S.A. 1947, §§ 72-748, 72-752, 72-753; Acts 2003, No. 41, § 1.

§ 17-87-203. Powers and duties

The Arkansas State Board of Nursing shall have the following powers and responsibilities:

(1) (A) Promulgate whatever regulations it deems necessary for the implementation of this chapter.

(B) No regulation promulgated hereafter by the board shall be effective until reviewed by the Legislative Council and the House Interim Committee on Public Health, Welfare, and Labor and the Senate Interim Committee on Public Health, Welfare, and Labor or appropriate subcommittees thereof;

(2) Cause the prosecution of persons violating this chapter;

(3) Keep a record of all its proceedings;

(4) Make an annual report to the Governor;

(5) Employ personnel necessary for carrying out its functions;

(6) Study, review, develop, and recommend role levels of technical classes of nursing service and practice to state and federal health agencies and to public and private administrative bodies;

(7) Fix the time for holding its regular meetings;

(8) Prescribe minimum standards and approve curricula for educational programs preparing persons for licensure as registered nurses, advanced practice nurses, registered nurse practitioner nurses, licensed practical nurses, and licensed psychiatric technician nurses;

(9) Prescribe minimum standards and approve curricula for educational programs preparing persons for certification as medication assistive persons;

(10) Provide for surveys of such programs at such times as it deems necessary or at the request of the schools;

(11) Approve programs that meet the requirements of this chapter;

(12) Deny or withdraw approval from educational programs for failure to meet prescribed standards;

(13) Examine, certify, and renew the certification of qualified applicants for medication assistive persons;

(14) Examine, license, and renew the licenses of qualified applicants for professional nursing, practical nursing, and psychiatric technician nursing;

(15) License and renew the licenses of qualified applicants for registered nurse practitioner nursing and advanced practice nursing;

(16) Grant certificates of prescriptive authority to qualified advanced practice nurses;

(17) Convene an advisory committee as provided for in this chapter to assist with oversight of prescriptive authority;

(18) Convene an advisory committee as provided for in this chapter to assist with oversight of medication assistive persons;

(19) Establish the maximum number of medication assistive persons who may be supervised by a nurse; and

(20) Conduct disciplinary proceedings as provided for in this chapter.

History:

> Acts 1971, No. 432, § 4; 1979, No. 404, § 3; A.S.A. 1947, § 72-748; Acts 1995, No. 409, § 6; 1997, No. 179, § 13; 2005, No. 1423, § 2.

§ 17-87-204. Deposit of Funds

All funds received by the Arkansas State Board of Nursing shall be deposited in the State Treasury to the credit of the board.

History:

> Acts 1971, No. 432, § 14; 1979, No. 404, § 4; A.S.A. 1947, § 72-758.

--------------------------------*Law Offices of Lisa Douglas, PLLC*--------------------------------

§17-87-205 Prescriptive Authority Advisory Committee

(a) (1) The Prescriptive Authority Advisory Committee is created as an advisory committee to the Arkansas State Board of Nursing.

(2) The committee shall assist the board in implementing the provisions of this chapter regarding prescriptive authority.

(b) The board shall appoint five (5) members, to be approved by the Governor, who have the following qualifications:

(1) Three (3) members shall be advanced practice nurses holding certificates of prescriptive authority;

(2) One (1) member shall be a licensed physician who has been involved in a collaborative practice with a registered nurse practitioner for at least five (5) years; and

(3) One (1) member shall be a licensed pharmacist who has been in practice for at least five (5) years.

(c) Members shall serve three-year terms.

(d) The board may remove any committee member, after notice and hearing, for incapacity, incompetence, neglect of duty, or malfeasance in office.

(e) The members shall serve without compensation, but may receive expense reimbursement in accordance with § 25-16-901 et seq.

History:

Acts 1995, No. 409, § 7; 1997, No. 250, § 160.

19

§17-87-206. Subpoenas and Subpoena Duces Tecum

(a) The Arkansas State Board of Nursing shall have the power to issue subpoenas and subpoenas duces tecum in connection with both its investigations and hearings.

(b) A subpoena duces tecum may require any book, writing, document, or other paper or thing which is germane to an investigation or hearing conducted by the board to be transmitted to the board.

(c) (1) Service of a subpoena shall be as provided by law for the service of subpoenas in civil cases in the circuit courts of this state, and the fees and mileage of officers serving the subpoenas and of witnesses appearing in answer to the subpoenas shall be the same as provided by law for proceedings in civil cases in the circuit courts of this state.

(2) (A) The board shall issue a subpoena or subpoena duces tecum upon the request of any party to a hearing before the board.

(B) The fees and mileage of the officers serving the subpoena and of the witness shall be paid by the party at whose request a witness is subpoenaed.

(d) (1) In the event a person shall have been served with a subpoena or subpoena duces tecum as provided in this section and fails to comply therewith, the board may apply to the circuit court of the county in which the board is conducting its investigation or hearing for an order causing the arrest of the person and directing that the person be brought before the court.

(2) The court shall have the power to punish the disobedient person for contempt as provided by law in the trial of civil cases in the circuit courts of this state.

History:

Acts 1997, No. 894, § 1.

§ 17-87-207. Continuing Education

(a) (1) The Arkansas State Board of Nursing shall adopt rules setting minimum standards for continuing education to ensure that all licensed nurses remain informed about those technical and professional subjects which the board deems appropriate to nursing practice.

(2) The board shall not require more than twenty (20) hours of continuing education per year.

(b) The board shall make every effort to ensure that the continuing education programs are offered either within the nurse's workplace or at another place convenient to the nurse, whether through live presentation or distance learning.

(c) (1) The board shall adopt rules to prescribe the methods by which the minimum standards for continuing education may be satisfied.

(2) The failure of any licensed nurse to satisfy the minimum standards for continuing education shall be grounds for disciplinary action or nonrenewal of the nurse's license, or both.

History:

Acts 2001, No. 86, § 1.

SUBCHAPTER 3–LICENSING

§ 17-87-301. Registered Nurses

(a) Qualifications. Before taking the examination or before the issuance of a license by endorsement, an applicant for a license to practice professional nursing shall submit to the Arkansas State Board of Nursing written evidence, verified by oath, that the applicant:

(1) Is of good moral character;

(2) Has completed an approved high school course of study or the equivalent thereof as determined by the appropriate educational agency; and

(3) Has completed the required approved professional nursing education program.

(b) Issuance of License. A license to practice as a registered nurse may be issued:

(1) By Examination. The applicant shall be required to pass an examination in such subjects as the board may determine. Upon successfully passing the examination, the board shall issue to the applicant a license to practice professional nursing as a registered nurse;

(2) By Endorsement. The board may issue a license to practice professional nursing as a registered nurse by endorsement to an applicant who has been duly licensed as a registered nurse under the laws of another state, territory, or foreign country if, in the opinion of the board, the applicant meets the qualifications required of registered nurses in this state at the time of graduation and if the board so recommends.

(c) Nurses Registered Prior to March 29, 1971. Any person holding a license or certificate of registration to practice nursing as a registered nurse issued by the board which was valid on March 29, 1971, shall be deemed to be licensed as a registered nurse under the provisions of this chapter.

(d) Title and Abbreviation. Any person who holds a license to practice professional nursing in this state shall have the right to use the title "registered nurse" and the abbreviation "R.N.".

History:

Acts 1971, No. 432, § 10; 1979, No. 613, § 3; 1981 (Ex. Sess.), No. 19, §§ 1-3; A.S.A. 1947, § 72-754; Acts 1991, No. 162, § 1; 1995, No. 409, § 8.

§ 17-87-302. Advanced Practice Nurses

(a) Qualifications. In order to be licensed as an advanced practice nurse, an applicant must show evidence of education approved by the Arkansas State Board of Nursing, and national certification approved by the board under one (1) of the following:

(1) Advanced Registered Nurse Practitioner. In order to qualify as an advanced registered nurse practitioner, an applicant must be currently certified as a nurse practitioner by a nationally recognized certifying body;

(2) Certified Registered Nurse Anesthetist. To qualify as a certified registered nurse anesthetist, an applicant must:

(A) Have earned a diploma or certificate evidencing satisfactory completion, beyond generic nursing preparation, of a formal educational program that meets the standards of the Council on Accreditation of Nurse Anesthesia Educational Programs or another nationally recognized accrediting body and that has as its objective the preparation of nurses to perform as nurse anesthetists; and

(B) Hold current certification from the Council on Certification of Nurse Anesthetists, the Council on Recertification of Nurse Anesthetists, or other nationally recognized certifying body;

(3) Certified Nurse Midwife. To qualify as a certified nurse midwife, an applicant must:

(A) Hold current certification as a nurse midwife from the American College of Nurse Midwives or other nationally recognized certifying body; and

(B) Have an agreement with a consulting physician if providing intrapartum care;

(4) Clinical Nurse Specialist. In order to qualify as a clinical nurse specialist, an applicant must hold a master's degree evidencing successful completion of a graduate program in nursing, which shall include supervised clinical practice and classroom instruction in a nursing specialty, and must be nationally certified in a specialty role as a clinical nurse specialist.

(b) Issuance of License. A license to practice as an advanced practice nurse may be issued:

(1) By Application. Any person holding a license to practice as a registered nurse and meeting the educational qualifications and certification requirements to be licensed as an advanced practice nurse may, upon application and payment of necessary fees to the board, be licensed as an advanced practice nurse; and

(2) By Endorsement. The board may issue a license to practice advanced practice nursing by endorsement to any applicant who has been licensed as an advanced practice nurse or to a person entitled to perform similar services under a different title under the laws of another state, territory, or foreign country if, in the opinion of the board, the applicant meets the requirements for advanced practice nurses in this state.

(c) Title and Abbreviation. Any person who holds a license to practice as an advanced practice nurse shall have the right to use the title of "advanced practice nurse" and the abbreviation "A.P.N.".

History:

Acts 1971, No. 432, § 2; 1979, No. 404, §§ 1, 7; 1979, No. 613, § 2; 1980 (1st Ex. Sess.), No. 14, §§ 5, 6; 1981 (Ex. Sess.), No. 19, § 8; A.S.A. 1947, §§ 72-746, 72-756.1, 72-756.2; Acts 1995, No. 409, § 9; 1999, No. 1208, § 2.

§17-87-303. Registered Nurse Practitioners

(a) (1) Any person holding a license to practice as a registered nurse and possessing the educational qualifications required under subsection (b) of this section to be licensed as a registered nurse practitioner may, upon application and payment of necessary fees to the Arkansas State Board of Nursing, be licensed as a registered nurse practitioner and have the right to use the title of "registered nurse practitioner" and the abbreviation "R.N.P.".

(2) No other person shall assume such a title or use such an abbreviation or any other words, letters, signs, or devices to indicate that the person using them is a registered nurse practitioner.

(b) In order to be licensed as a registered nurse practitioner, a registered nurse must hold a certificate or academic degree evidencing successful completion of the educational program of an accredited school of nursing or other nationally recognized accredited program recognized by the board as meeting the requirements of a nurse practitioner program.

(c) However, any person qualified to receive a license as a registered nurse practitioner may obtain the license upon the payment of a fee not to exceed twenty-five dollars ($25.00) for the original license. The license fees are to be in addition to the person's registered nurse license fees.

History:

Acts 1971, No. 432, §§ 2, 10; 1979, No. 404, §§ 1, 7; 1979, No. 613, §§ 2, 3; 1981 (Ex. Sess.), No. 19, §§ 1-3; A.S.A. 1947, §§ 72-746, 72-754.

§ 17-87-304. Licensed Practical Nurses

(a) Qualifications. An applicant for a license to practice practical nursing shall submit to the Arkansas State Board of Nursing evidence, verified by oath, that the applicant:

(1) Is of good moral character;

(2) Has completed an approved high school course of study or the equivalent thereof as determined by the appropriate educational agency; and

(3) Has completed a prescribed curriculum in a state-approved program for the preparation of practical nurses and holds a diploma or certificate therefrom. However, the Arkansas State Board of Nursing may waive this requirement if the board determines the applicant to be otherwise qualified.

(b) Issuance of License. A license to practice as a practical nurse may be issued:

(1) By Examination. The applicant shall be required to pass an examination in such subjects as the board may determine. Upon successful completion of the examination, the board shall issue to the applicant a license to practice as a licensed practical nurse;

(2) By Endorsement. The board may issue a license to practice practical nursing by endorsement to any applicant who has duly been licensed or registered as a licensed practical nurse or to a person entitled to perform similar services under a different title under the laws of another state, territory, or foreign country if, in the opinion of the board, the applicant meets the requirements for licensed practical nurses in this state at the time of graduation and if the board so recommends.

(c) Person Licensed Prior to March 29, 1971. Any person holding a license to practice as a practical nurse issued by the board and which was valid on March 29, 1971, shall be deemed to be licensed as a practical nurse under the provisions of this chapter.

(d) Title and Abbreviation. Any person who holds a license to practice practical nursing in this state shall have the right to use the title "licensed practical nurse" and the abbreviation "L.P.N.".

History:

Acts 1971, No. 432, § 11; 1981, No. 54, § 1; 1981 (Ex. Sess.), No. 19, §§ 4, 5; A.S.A. 1947, § 72-755; Acts 1991, No. 162, § 2; 1995, No. 409, § 10.

§ 17-87-305. Licensed Psychiatric Technician Nurses

(a) Qualifications. An applicant for a license to practice psychiatric technician nursing shall submit to the Arkansas State Board of Nursing evidence, verified by oath, that the applicant:

(1) Is of good moral character;

(2) Has completed an approved high school course of study or the equivalent thereof as determined by the appropriate educational agency; and

(3) Has completed a prescribed curriculum in a state-approved program for the preparation of psychiatric technician nurses and holds a diploma or certificate therefrom. However, the board may waive this requirement if the board determines the applicant to be otherwise qualified.

(b) Issuance of License. A license to practice as a psychiatric technician nurse may be issued:

(1) By Examination. The applicant shall be required to pass a written examination in such subjects as the board may determine. Each written examination may be supplemented by an oral examination. Upon successfully passing the examination, the board shall issue to the applicant a license to practice as a psychiatric technician nurse. All such examinations shall be conducted by an examiner, who shall be a registered nurse, and by an assistant examiner, who shall be a licensed psychiatric technician nurse;

(2) By Endorsement. The board may issue a license to practice psychiatric technician nursing by endorsement to an applicant who has duly been licensed or registered as a licensed psychiatric technician nurse or a person entitled to perform similar services under a different title under the laws of another state, territory, or foreign country if, in the opinion of the board, the applicant meets the requirements for licensed psychiatric technician nurses in this state at the time of graduation and if the board so recommends.

(c) Person Licensed Prior to March 29, 1971. Any person holding a license to practice as a psychiatric technician issued by the board in accordance with Acts 1953, No. 124 (repealed), and which was valid on March 29, 1971, shall be deemed to be licensed as a psychiatric technician nurse under the provisions of this chapter.

(d) Title and Abbreviation. Any person who holds a license to practice psychiatric technician nursing in this state shall have the right to use the title "licensed psychiatric technician nurse" and the abbreviation "L.P.T.N.".

History: Acts 1971, No. 432, § 12; 1981, No. 54, § 2; 1981 (Ex. Sess.), No. 19, §§ 6, 7; A.S.A. 1947, § 72-756; Acts 1995, No. 409, § 11.

§ 17-87-306.   Fees

The Arkansas State Board of Nursing shall establish and collect fees and penalties for services relating to certification, examination, licensing, endorsement, certification for prescriptive authority, temporary permits, license renewal, certification renewal, and other reasonable services as determined by the board.

History:

Acts 1995, No. 409, § 12; 2005, No. 1423, § 3.

§17-87-307.   Temporary Permits

(a) (1) Upon application and payment of the required fee, the Arkansas State Board of Nursing may issue a temporary permit to practice professional, practical, or psychiatric technician nursing to a qualified applicant who has:

(A) Completed a program in professional, practical, or psychiatric technician nursing approved by the appropriate state or national authorizing agency of this state or country and by the appropriate authorizing agency of other states or territories or foreign countries; and

(B) Applied for or is awaiting results of the first examination he or she is eligible to take after the permit is issued.

(2) The permit shall become invalid upon notification to the applicant of the results of the first examination he or she is eligible to take after the permit is issued.

(b) (1) Upon application and payment of the required fee, the board shall issue a temporary permit to a qualified applicant holding a current professional, practical, or psychiatric technician license from another jurisdiction from any other state or territory awaiting endorsement.

(2) This permit must have an issuance date and an expiration date. The permit shall be valid for no more than six (6) months.

(c) (1) Upon application and payment of the required fee, an applicant shall be issued a temporary permit to practice advanced practice nursing who has:

(A) Satisfactorily completed an educational program for advanced practice nursing approved by the board; and

(B) Been accepted by the appropriate certification body to sit for the first national certification exam he or she is eligible to take.

(2) The permit shall expire upon notification to the applicant of the results of the examination.

(3) The permit is not renewable and does not apply to prescriptive authority.

(d) (1) Upon application and payment of the required fee, the board shall issue a temporary permit to a qualified applicant holding a current advanced practice nurse license or the equivalent from another jurisdiction from any other state or territory awaiting endorsement.

(2) (A) This permit must have an issuance date and a date when it shall become invalid.

(B) The permit shall automatically become invalid upon notification of the applicant's failure to pass the appropriate national certification exam.

(C) In no event shall the permit be valid in excess of six (6) months.

History:

Acts 1971, No. 432, § 13; 1977, No. 88, § 1; 1979, No. 90, § 1; 1980 (1st Ex. Sess.), No. 14, § 2; 1981 (Ex. Sess.), No. 19, § 9; A.S.A. 1947, § 72-757; Acts 1995, No. 409, § 13; 2001, No. 303, § 1

§ 17-87-308.   Renewal of Licenses

(a) (1) The Arkansas State Board of Nursing shall prescribe the procedure for the cyclical biennial renewal of licenses to every person licensed by the board.

(2) In each case, the board shall mail a notification for renewal to the licensee at least thirty (30) days prior to the expiration date of the license.

(b) Upon receipt of the application and the fee, the board shall verify the accuracy of the application and renew the license for a period to expire on the last day of the current biennial cycle.

(c) The renewal shall render the holder a legal practitioner of nursing for the period stated in subsection (b) of this section.

(d) Any licensee who allows his or her license to lapse by failing to renew the license as provided in this section may be reinstated by the board on payment of the renewal fee plus a penalty.

(e) Any person practicing nursing during the time his or her license has lapsed shall be considered an illegal practitioner and shall be subject to the penalties provided for violations of this chapter.

(f) (1) (A) An individual may place his or her license on inactive status with written notification to the board.

(B) The holder of an inactive license shall not practice nursing in this state.

(2) (A) The provisions relating to the denial, suspension, and revocation of a license shall be applicable to an inactive or lapsed license.

(B) When proceedings to suspend or revoke an inactive license or otherwise discipline the holder of an inactive license have been initiated, the license shall not be reinstated until the proceedings have been completed.

(3) An inactive license may be placed in an active status upon compliance with the rules established by the board.

(g) As a condition of licensure renewal, an advanced practice nurse shall submit proof of current national certification and successful completion of continuing education as required by the board.

History: Acts 1971, No. 432, § 13; 1981 (Ex. Sess.), No. 19, § 9; A.S.A. 1947, § 72-757; Acts 1987, No. 147, § 1; 1995, No. 409, § 14; 1997, No. 179, § 14; 2005, No. 61,

§ 17-87-309. Disciplinary Actions

(a) The Arkansas State Board of Nursing shall have sole authority to deny, suspend, revoke, or limit any license or privilege to practice nursing or certificate of prescriptive authority issued by the board or applied for in accordance with the provisions of this chapter or to otherwise discipline a licensee upon proof that the person:

(1) Is guilty of fraud or deceit in procuring or attempting to procure a license to practice nursing or is engaged in the practice of nursing without a valid license;

(2) Is guilty of a crime or gross immorality;

(3) Is unfit or incompetent by reason of negligence, habits, or other causes;

(4) Is habitually intemperate or is addicted to the use of habit-forming drugs;

(5) Is mentally incompetent;

(6) Is guilty of unprofessional conduct;

(7) Has had a license, privilege to practice, certificate, or registration revoked or suspended or has been placed on probation or under disciplinary order in any jurisdiction;

(8) Has voluntarily surrendered a license, privilege to practice, certification, or registration and has not been reinstated in any jurisdiction; or

(9) Has willfully or repeatedly violated any of the provisions of this chapter.

(b) The board shall refuse to issue or shall revoke the license of any person who is found guilty of or pleads guilty or nolo contendere to any offense listed in § 17-87-312(f), unless the person requests and the board grants a waiver pursuant to § 17-87-312(h).

(c) Proceedings under this section shall be as provided in the Arkansas Administrative Procedure Act, § 25-15-201 et seq.

History:

Acts 1971, No. 432, § 16; A.S.A. 1947, § 72-760; Acts 1995, No. 409, § 15; 1999, No. 1208, § 3; 2001, No. 212, § 1; 2007, No. 207, § 1.

§ 17-87-310. Prescriptive Authority

 (a) The Arkansas State Board of Nursing may grant a certificate of prescriptive authority to an advanced practice nurse who:

 (1) Submits proof of successful completion of a board-approved advanced pharmacology course that shall include preceptorial experience in the prescription of drugs, medicines, and therapeutic devices; and

 (2) Has a collaborative practice agreement with a physician who is licensed under the Arkansas Medical Practices Act, §§ 17-95-201 — 17-95-207, 17-95-301 — 17-95-305, and 17-95-401 — 17-95-411, and who has a practice comparable in scope, specialty, or expertise to that of the advanced practice nurse on file with the board.

 (b) (1) An advanced practice nurse with a certificate of prescriptive authority may receive and prescribe drugs, medicines, or therapeutic devices appropriate to the advanced practice nurse's area of practice in accordance with rules established by the board.

 (2) An advanced practice nurse's prescriptive authority shall only extend to drugs listed in Schedules III — V.

 (c) A collaborative practice agreement shall include, but not be limited to, provisions addressing:

 (1) The availability of the collaborating physician for consultation or referral, or both;

 (2) Methods of management of the collaborative practice, which shall include protocols for prescriptive authority;

 (3) Coverage of the health care needs of a patient in the emergency absence of the advanced practice nurse or physician; and

 (4) Quality assurance.

 (d) If a collaborative practice results in complaints of violations of the Arkansas Medical Practices Act, §§ 17-95-201 — 17-95-207, 17-95-301 — 17-95-305, and 17-95-401 — 17-95-411, the Arkansas State Medical Board may review the role of the physician in the collaborative practice to determine if the physician is unable to manage his or her responsibilities under the agreement without an adverse affect on the quality of care of the patient.

 (e) If a collaborative practice results in complaints of violations of this chapter,

the Arkansas State Board of Nursing may review the role of the advanced practice nurse in the collaborative practice to determine if the nurse is unable to manage his or her responsibilities under the agreement without an adverse affect on the quality of care of the patient.

History:

Acts 1995, No. 409, § 16.

§ 17-87-311. Direct Reimbursement Agreements

(a) An advanced practice nurse or a registered nurse practitioner may enter into a direct reimbursement agreement with the agency administering the state medicaid program.

(b) The agency administering the state medicaid program shall not discriminate against practitioners providing covered services within the scope of their practice based on the type of practitioner.

History:

Acts 1995, No. 409, § 17.

§ 17-87-312. Criminal Background Checks

(a) Each first-time applicant for a license issued by the Arkansas State Board of Nursing shall apply to the Identification Bureau of the Department of Arkansas State Police for a state and national criminal background check, to be conducted by the Federal Bureau of Investigation.

(b) The check shall conform to the applicable federal standards and shall include the taking of fingerprints.

(c) The applicant shall sign a release of information to the board and shall be responsible to the Department of Arkansas State Police for the payment of any fee associated with the criminal background check.

(d) Upon completion of the criminal background check, the Identification Bureau of the Department of Arkansas State Police shall forward to the board all information obtained concerning the applicant in the commission of any offense listed in subsection (e) of this section.

(e) Except as provided in subdivision (l)(1) of this section, no person shall be eligible to receive or hold a license issued by the board if that person has pleaded guilty or nolo contendere to or has been found guilty of any of the following offenses by any court in the State of Arkansas or of any similar offense by a court in another state or of any similar offense by a federal court:

(1) Capital murder as prohibited in § 5-10-101;

(2) Murder in the first degree as prohibited in § 5-10-102 and murder in the second degree as prohibited in § 5-10-103;

(3) Manslaughter as prohibited in § 5-10-104;

(4) Negligent homicide as prohibited in § 5-10-105;

(5) Kidnaping as prohibited in § 5-11-102;

(6) False imprisonment in the first degree as prohibited in § 5-11-103;

(7) Permanent detention or restraint as prohibited in § 5-11-106;

(8) Robbery as prohibited in § 5-12-102;

(9) Aggravated robbery as prohibited in § 5-12-103;

(10) Battery in the first degree as prohibited in § 5-13-201;

(11) Aggravated assault as prohibited in § 5-13-204;

(12) Introduction of a controlled substance into the body of another person as prohibited in § 5-13-210;

(13) Terroristic threatening in the first degree as prohibited in § 5-13-301;

(14) Rape as prohibited in § 5-14-103;

(15) Sexual indecency with a child as prohibited in § 5-14-110;

(16) Sexual assault in the first degree, second degree, third degree, and fourth degree as prohibited in §§ 5-14-124 — 5-14-127;

(17) Incest as prohibited in § 5-26-202;

(18) Offenses against the family as prohibited in §§ 5-26-303 — 5-26-306;

(19) Endangering the welfare of an incompetent person in the first degree as prohibited in § 5-27-201;

(20) Endangering the welfare of a minor in the first degree as prohibited in § 5-27-205;

(21) Permitting abuse of a minor as prohibited in § 5-27-221(a)(1) and (3);

(22) Engaging children in sexually explicit conduct for use in visual or print media, transportation of minors for prohibited sexual conduct, pandering or possessing visual or print medium depicting sexually explicit conduct involving a child, or use of a child or consent to use of a child in a sexual performance by producing, directing, or promoting a sexual performance by a child as prohibited in §§ 5-27-303 — 5-27-305, 5-27-402, and 5-27-403;

(23) Felony adult abuse as prohibited in § 5-28-103;

(24) Theft of property as prohibited in § 5-36-103;

(25) Theft by receiving as prohibited in § 5-36-106;

(26) Arson as prohibited in § 5-38-301;

(27) Burglary as prohibited in § 5-39-201;

(28) Felony violation of the Uniform Controlled Substances Act, §§ 5-64-101 — 5-64-608 as prohibited in § 5-64-401;

(29) Promotion of prostitution in the first degree as prohibited in § 5-70-104;

(30) Stalking as prohibited in § 5-71-229;

(31) Criminal attempt, criminal complicity, criminal solicitation, or criminal conspiracy as prohibited in §§ 5-3-201, 5-3-202, 5-3-301, and 5-3-401, to commit any of the offenses listed in this subsection;

(32) Computer child pornography as prohibited in § 5-27-603; and

(33) Computer exploitation of a child in the first degree as prohibited in § 5-27-605.

(f) (1) (A) The board may issue a nonrenewable temporary permit for licensure to a first-time applicant pending the results of the criminal background check.

        (B) The permit shall be valid for no more than six (6) months.

        (2) Except as provided in subdivision (l)(1) of this section, upon receipt of information from the Identification Bureau of the Department of Arkansas State Police that the person holding the letter of provisional licensure has pleaded guilty or nolo contendere to, or has been found guilty of, any offense listed in subsection (e) of this section, the board shall immediately revoke the provisional license.

        (g) (1) The provisions of subsection (e) and subdivision (f)(2) of this section may be waived by the board upon the request of:

        (A) An affected applicant for licensure; or

        (B) The person holding a license subject to revocation.

        (2) Circumstances for which a waiver may be granted shall include, but not be limited to, the following:

        (A) The age at which the crime was committed;

        (B) The circumstances surrounding the crime;

        (C) The length of time since the crime;

        (D) Subsequent work history;

        (E) Employment references;

        (F) Character references; and

        (G) Other evidence demonstrating that the applicant does not pose a threat to the health or safety of the public.

        (h) (1) Any information received by the board from the Identification Bureau of the Department of Arkansas State Police pursuant to this section shall not be available for examination except by:

        (A) The affected applicant for licensure or his or her authorized representative; or

        (B) The person whose license is subject to revocation or his or her authorized representative.

        (2) No record, file, or document shall be removed from the custody of the

Department of Arkansas State Police.

(i) Any information made available to the affected applicant for licensure or the person whose license is subject to revocation shall be information pertaining to that person only.

(j) Rights of privilege and confidentiality established in this section shall not extend to any document created for purposes other than this background check.

(k) The board shall adopt the necessary rules and regulations to fully implement the provisions of this section.

(l) (1) For purposes of this section, an expunged record of a conviction or a plea of guilty or nolo contendere to an offense listed in subsection (e) of this section shall not be considered a conviction, guilty plea, or nolo contendere plea to the offense unless the offense is also listed in subdivision (l)(2) of this section.

(2) Because of the serious nature of the offenses and the close relationship to the type of work that is to be performed, the following shall result in permanent disqualification:

(A) Capital murder as prohibited in § 5-10-101;

(B) Murder in the first degree as prohibited in § 5-10-102 and murder in the second degree as prohibited in § 5-10-103;

(C) Kidnaping as prohibited in § 5-11-102;

(D) Rape as prohibited in § 5-14-103;

(E) Sexual assault in the first degree as prohibited in § 5-14-124 and sexual assault in the second degree as prohibited in § 5-14-125;

(F) Endangering the welfare of a minor in the first degree as prohibited in § 5-27-205 and endangering the welfare of a minor in the second degree as prohibited in § 5-27-206;

(G) Incest as prohibited in § 5-26-202;

(H) Arson as prohibited in § 5-38-301;

(I) Endangering the welfare of an incompetent person in the first degree as prohibited in § 5-27-201; and

(J) Adult abuse that constitutes a felony as prohibited in § 5-28-103.

History: Acts 1999, No. 1208, § 4; 2001, No. 303, §§ 2-4; 2003, No. 103, §§ 1, 2; No. 1087, § 15; No. 1386, § 1; No. 1449, § 1; 2005, No. 1923, § 2.

SUBCHAPTER 4 - EDUCATIONAL PROGRAMS

§ 17-87-401. Nursing Education Programs

(a) An institution desiring to conduct a nursing education program to prepare professional, advanced practice, nurse practitioner, practical, and psychiatric technician nurses shall apply to the Arkansas State Board of Nursing and submit evidence that:

(1) It is prepared to carry out a program in professional nursing education, advanced practice nursing education, nurse practitioner nursing education, practical nursing education, or psychiatric technician nursing training, as the case may be; and

(2) It is prepared to meet such standards as shall be established by this chapter and by the board.

(b) (1) A survey of the institution and its entire nursing education program shall be made by an authorized representative of the board, who shall submit a written report of the survey to the board.

(2) If, in the opinion of the board, the requirements for an approved nursing education program are met, the program shall be approved as a nursing education program for professional, advanced practice, nurse practitioner, practical, and psychiatric technician nurses.

(c) (1) From time to time, as deemed necessary, it shall be the duty of the board, through its authorized representative, to survey its nursing education programs in the state.

(2) Written reports of such surveys shall be submitted to the board.

(3) If the board shall determine that any approved nursing education program under its supervision is not maintaining the standards required by the statutes and by the board, notice thereof in writing specifying the defect or defects shall be immediately given to the institution conducting the program.

(4) A program which fails within a reasonable time to correct these conditions to the satisfaction of the board shall be withdrawn after a hearing.

History: Acts 1971, No. 432, § 15; A.S.A. 1947, § 72-759; Acts 1995, No. 409, § 18.

§ 17-87-402. Institutions of Higher Education-Challenge and Validation Examinations

(a) As used in this section, unless the context otherwise requires:

(1) "Challenge examination" means a test designed to determine the level of knowledge of the person being tested in the subject area of the test. Challenge examinations may cover any area of academic pursuit; and

(2) "Validation examination" means an evaluation of prior knowledge, experience, or skills. Validation examinations are administered to determine the proper placement of the examinee within the nurse training program.

(b) The Department of Higher Education shall:

(1) Encourage and supervise the development of methods of validation of nursing knowledge and skills through written and clinical testing mechanisms;

(2) Review and approve validation and challenge examinations for fairness and relevant content;

(3) Set uniform passing scores to be used by institutions of higher education in this state for passing standardized validation and challenge examinations when the passing scores are not determined at the national level; and

(4) Require schools using individual school-made tests to select one (1) standard passing score for each test which any level of student must achieve to receive credit.

(c) All institutions of higher education in this state shall use standardized validation and challenge examinations or devise their own. All challenge examinations and all validation examinations shall be submitted to the Department of Higher Education for its approval. Upon the successful passing of a validation examination or challenge examination, the examinee shall be given credit for the course which is the subject of the test.

(d) Each Arkansas institution of higher education shall accept the credit given by other Arkansas institutions of higher education for the successful passing of a challenge examination or a validation examination on any course required in the nursing curriculum.

(e) (1) Licensed practical nurses and licensed psychiatric technician nurses may transfer or challenge by test, or validate, up to thirty (30) semester credit hours from the total nursing program curriculum upon entering diploma, associate degree, or baccalaureate degree programs in nursing in Arkansas. This does not include other hours they may have earned which may also be transferred.

(2) Registered nurses may transfer or challenge by test, or validate, up to sixty (60) semester credit hours from the total nursing program curriculum upon entering a baccalaureate degree program in nursing in Arkansas. This does not include other hours they may have earned which may also be transferred.

History:

Acts 1979, No. 88, §§ 1-5; A.S.A. 1947, §§ 72-759.1 — 72-759.5.

§ 17-87-403. Nursing Recruitment and Admission

Upon request, the Arkansas State Board of Nursing shall provide assistance to publicly supported institutions of higher education in implementing programs offered under § 6-60-212.

History:

Acts 2005, No. 1256, § 2.

SUBCHAPTER 6-NURSE LICENSURE COMPACT

§ 17-87-601. Text of Compact

The Interstate Nurse Licensure Compact is enacted into law and entered into by this state with all states legally joining therein and in the form substantially as follows:

NURSE LICENSURE COMPACT

ARTICLE I
Findings and Declaration of Purpose

(a) The party states find that:

(1) The health and safety of the public are affected by the degree of compliance with and the effectiveness of enforcement activities related to state nurse licensure laws;

(2) Violations of nurse licensure and other laws regulating the practice of nursing may result in injury or harm to the public;

(3) The expanded mobility of nurses and the use of advanced communication technologies as part of our nation's healthcare delivery system require greater coordination and cooperation among states in the areas of nurse licensure and regulation;

(4) New practice modalities and technology make compliance with individual state nurse licensure laws difficult and complex; and

(5) The current system of duplicative licensure for nurses practicing in multiple states is cumbersome and redundant to both nurses and states.

(b) The general purposes of this Compact are to:

(1) Facilitate the states' responsibility to protect the public's health and safety;

(2) Ensure and encourage the cooperation of party states in the areas of nurse licensure and regulation;

(3) Facilitate the exchange of information between party states in the areas of nurse regulation, investigation, and adverse actions;

(4) Promote compliance with the laws governing the practice of nursing in each jurisdiction;

(5) Invest all party states with the authority to hold a nurse accountable for meeting all state practice laws in the state in which the patient is located at the time care is rendered through the mutual recognition of party state licenses.

.

ARTICLE II
Definitions

As used in this Compact:

(1) "Adverse action" means a home or remote state action;

(2) "Alternative program" means a voluntary, nondisciplinary monitoring program approved by a nurse licensing board;

(3) "Coordinated Licensure Information System" means an integrated process for collecting, storing, and sharing information on nurse licensure and enforcement activities related to nurse licensure laws, which is administered by a non-profit organization composed of and controlled by state nurse licensing boards;

(4) "Current significant investigative information" means:

(A) Investigative information that a licensing board after a preliminary inquiry that includes notification and an opportunity for the nurse to respond if required by state law, has reason to believe is not groundless and, if proved true, would indicate more than a minor infraction; or

(B) Investigative information that indicates that the nurse represents an immediate threat to public health and safety regardless of whether the nurse has been notified and had an opportunity to respond;

(5) "Home state" means the party state which is the nurse's primary state of residence;

(6) "Home state action" means any administrative, civil, equitable or criminal action permitted by the home state's laws which are imposed on a nurse by the home state's licensing board or other authority including actions against an individual's license such as: revocation, suspension, probation, or any other action which affects a nurse's authorization to practice;

(7) "Licensing board" means a party state's regulatory body responsible for issuing nurse licenses;

(8) "Multistate licensure privilege" means current, official authority from a remote state permitting the practice of nursing as either a registered nurse or a licensed practical/vocational nurse in such party state. All party states have the authority, in accordance with existing state due process law, to take actions against the nurse's privilege such as: revocation, suspension, probation, or any other action which affects a nurse's authorization to practice;

(9) "Nurse" means a registered nurse or licensed practical/vocational nurse, as those terms are defined by each party's state practice laws;

(10) "Party state" means any state that has adopted this Compact;

(11) "Remote state" means a party state, other than the home state:

    (A) Where the patient is located at the time nursing care is provided; or

    (B) In the case of the practice of nursing not involving a patient, in such party state where the recipient of nursing practice is located;

(12) "Remote state action" means:

    (A) Any administrative, civil, equitable, or criminal action permitted by a remote state's laws which are imposed on a nurse by the remote state's licensing board or other authority including actions against an individual's multistate licensure privilege to practice in the remote state; and

    (B) Cease and desist and other injunctive or equitable orders issued by remote states or the licensing boards thereof;

(13) "State" means a state, territory, or possession of the United States, the District of Columbia, or the Commonwealth of Puerto Rico; and

(14) "State practice laws" means those individual party's state laws and regulations that govern the practice of nursing, define the scope of nursing practice, and create the methods and grounds for imposing discipline. "State practice laws" does not include the initial qualifications for licensure or requirements necessary to obtain and retain a license, except for qualifications or requirements of the home state.

ARTICLE III

General Provisions and Jurisdiction

(a) A license to practice registered nursing issued by a home state to a resident in that state will be recognized by each party state as authorizing a multistate licensure privilege to practice as a registered nurse in such party state. A license to practice licensed practical/vocational nursing issued by a home state to a resident in that state will be recognized by each party state as authorizing a multistate licensure privilege to practice as a licensed practical/vocational nurse in such party state. In order to obtain or retain a license, an applicant must meet the home state's qualifications for licensure and license renewal as well as all other applicable state laws.

(b) Party states may, in accordance with state due process laws, limit or revoke the multistate licensure privilege of any nurse to practice in their states and may take any other actions under their applicable state laws necessary to protect the health and safety of their citizens. If a party state takes such action, it shall promptly notify the administrator of the coordinated licensure information system. The administrator of the coordinated licensure information system shall promptly notify the home state of any such actions by remote states.

(c) Every nurse practicing in a party state must comply with the state practice laws of the state in which the patient is located at the time care is rendered. In addition, the practice of nursing is not limited to patient care, but shall include all nursing practice as defined by the state practice laws of a party state. The practice of nursing will subject a nurse to the jurisdiction of the nurse licensing board and the courts, as well as the laws, in that party state.

(d) This Compact does not affect additional requirements imposed by states for advanced practice registered nursing. However, a multistate licensure privilege to practice registered nursing granted by a party state shall be recognized by other party states as a license to practice registered nursing if one is required by state law as a precondition for qualifying for advanced practice registered nurse authorization.

(e) Individuals not residing in a party state shall continue to be able to apply for nurse licensure as provided for under the laws of each party state. However, the license granted to these individuals will not be recognized as granting the privilege to practice nursing in any other party state unless explicitly agreed to by that party state.

ARTICLE IV

Applications for Licensure in a Party State

(a) Upon application for a license, the licensing board in a party state shall ascertain, through the coordinated licensure information system, whether the applicant has ever held, or is the holder of, a license issued by any other state, whether there are any restrictions on the multistate licensure privilege, and whether any other adverse action by any state has been taken against the license.

(b) A nurse in a party state shall hold licensure in only one (1) party state at a time, issued by the home state.

(c) A nurse who intends to change primary state of residence may apply for licensure in the new home state in advance of such change. However, new licenses will not be issued by a party state until after a nurse provides evidence of change in primary state of residence satisfactory to the new home state's licensing board.

(d) When a nurse changes primary state of residence by:

(1) Moving between two party states, and obtains a license from the new home state, the license from the former home state is no longer valid;

(2) Moving from a nonparty state to a party state, and obtains a license from the new home state, the individual state license issued by the nonparty state is not affected and will remain in full force if so provided by the laws of the nonparty state;

(3) Moving from a party state to a nonparty state, the license issued by the prior home state converts to an individual state license, valid only in the former home state, without the multistate licensure privilege to practice in other party states.

ARTICLE V
Adverse Actions

In addition to the General Provisions described in Article III, the following provisions apply:

(1) The licensing board of a remote state shall promptly report to the administrator of the coordinated licensure information system any remote state actions including the factual and legal basis for such action, if known. The licensing board of a remote state shall also promptly report any significant current investigative information yet to result in a remote state action. The administrator of the coordinated licensure information system shall promptly notify the home state of any such reports;

(2) The licensing board of a party state shall have the authority to complete any pending investigations for a nurse who changes primary state of residence during the course of such investigations. It shall also have the authority to take appropriate action(s), and shall promptly report the conclusions of such investigations to the administrator of the coordinated licensure information system. The administrator of the coordinated licensure information system shall promptly notify the new home state of any such actions;

(3) A remote state may take adverse action affecting the multistate licensure privilege to practice within that party state. However, only the home state shall have the power to impose adverse action against the license issued by the home state;

(4) For purposes of imposing adverse action, the licensing board of the home state shall give the same priority and effect to reported conduct received from a remote state as it would if such conduct had occurred within the home state. In so doing, it shall apply its own state laws to determine appropriate action;

(5) The home state may take adverse action based on the factual findings of the remote state, so long as each state follows its own procedures for imposing such adverse action; and

(6) Nothing in this Compact shall override a party state's decision that participation in an alternative program may be used in lieu of licensure action and that such participation shall remain nonpublic if required by the party state's laws. Party states must require nurses who enter any alternative programs to agree not to practice in any other party state during the term of the alternative program without prior authorization from such other party state.

ARTICLE VI

Additional Authorities Invested in Party State Nurse Licensing Boards

Notwithstanding any other powers, party state nurse licensing boards shall have the authority to:

(1) If otherwise permitted by state law, recover from the affected nurse the costs of investigations and disposition of cases resulting from any adverse action taken against that nurse;

(2) Issue subpoenas for both hearings and investigations which require the attendance and testimony of witnesses, and the production of evidence. Subpoenas issued by a nurse licensing board in a party state for the attendance and testimony of witnesses, and/or the production of evidence from another party state, shall be enforced in the latter state by any court of competent jurisdiction, according to the practice and procedure of that court applicable to subpoenas issued in proceedings pending before it. The issuing authority shall pay any witness fees, travel expenses, mileage and other fees required by the service statutes of the state where the witnesses and/or evidence are located;

(3) Issue cease and desist orders to limit or revoke a nurse's authority to practice in their state; and

(4) Promulgate uniform rules and regulations as provided for in Article VIII(c).

ARTICLE VII

Coordinated Licensure Information System

(a) All party states shall participate in a cooperative effort to create a coordinated database of all licensed registered nurses and licensed practical/vocational nurses. This system will include information on the licensure and disciplinary history of each nurse, as contributed by party states, to assist in the coordination of nurse licensure and enforcement efforts.

(b) Notwithstanding any other provision of law, all party states' licensing boards shall promptly report adverse actions, actions against multistate licensure privileges, any current significant investigative information yet to result in adverse action, denials of applications, and the reasons for such denials, to the coordinated licensure information system.

(c) Current significant investigative information shall be transmitted through the coordinated licensure information system only to party state licensing boards.

(d) Notwithstanding any other provision of law, all party states' licensing boards contributing information to the coordinated licensure information system may designate information that may not be shared with nonparty states or disclosed to other entities or individuals without the express permission of the contributing state.

(e) Any personally identifiable information obtained by a party states' licensing board from the coordinated licensure information system may not be shared with nonparty states or disclosed to other entities or individuals except to the extent permitted by the laws of the party state contributing the information.

(f) Any information contributed to the coordinated licensure information system that is subsequently required to be expunged by the laws of the party states contributing that information, shall also be expunged from the coordinated licensure information system.

(g) The compact administrators, acting jointly with each other and in consultation with the administrator of the coordinated licensure information system, shall formulate necessary and proper procedures for the identification, collection, and exchange of information under this Compact.

ARTICLE VIII

Compact Administration and Interchange of Information

(a) The head of the nurse licensing board, or his/her designee, of each party state shall be the administrator of this Compact for his/her state.

(b) The compact administrator of each party state shall furnish to the compact administrator of each other party state any information and documents including, but not limited to, a uniform data set of investigations, identifying information, licensure data, and disclosable alternative program participation information to facilitate the administration of this Compact.

(c) Compact administrators shall have the authority to develop uniform rules to facilitate and coordinate implementation of this Compact. These uniform rules shall be adopted by party states, under the authority invested under Article VI(d).

ARTICLE IX

Immunity

No party state or the officers or employees or agents of a party state's nurse licensing board who acts in accordance with the provisions of this Compact shall be liable on account of any act or omission in good faith while engaged in the performance of their duties under this Compact. Good faith in this article shall not include willful misconduct or gross negligence.

ARTICLE X

Entry into Force, Withdrawal and Amendment

(a) This Compact shall enter into force and become effective as to any state when it has been enacted into the laws of that state. Any party state may withdraw from this Compact by enacting a statute repealing the same, but no such withdrawal shall take effect until six (6) months after the withdrawing state has given notice of the withdrawal to the executive heads of all other party states.

(b) No withdrawal shall affect the validity or applicability by the licensing boards of states remaining party to the Compact of any report of adverse action occurring prior to the withdrawal.

(c) Nothing contained in this Compact shall be construed to invalidate or prevent any nurse licensure agreement or other cooperative arrangement between a party state and a nonparty state that is made in accordance with the other provisions of this Compact.

(d) This Compact may be amended by the party states. No amendment to this Compact shall become effective and binding upon the party states unless and until it is enacted into the laws of all party states.

ARTICLE XI

Construction and Severability

(a) This Compact shall be liberally construed so as to effectuate the purposes thereof. The provisions of this Compact shall be severable and if any phrase, clause, sentence, or provision of this Compact is declared to be contrary to the constitution of any party state or of the United States or the applicability thereof to any government, agency, person, or circumstance is held invalid, the validity of the remainder of this Compact and the applicability thereof to any government, agency, person, or circumstance shall not be affected thereby. If this Compact shall be held contrary to the constitution of any state party thereto, the Compact shall remain in full force and effect as to the remaining party states and in full force and effect as to the party state affected as to all severable matters.

(b) In the event party states find a need for settling disputes arising under this Compact:

(1) The party states may submit the issues in dispute to an arbitration panel which will be comprised of an individual appointed by the compact administrator in the home state; an individual appointed by the compact administrator in the remote state(s) involved; and an individual mutually agreed upon by the compact administrators of all the party states involved in the dispute; and

(2) The decision of a majority of the arbitrators shall be final and binding.

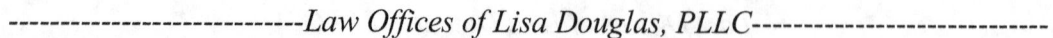

§17-87-602 Practice Privileges - Power of Board to Limit or Revoke

The Arkansas State Board of Nursing may limit or revoke practice privileges in this state of a person licensed to practice nursing by a jurisdiction that has joined the Compact or take action on previous practice privilege action from another party state.

History:

    Acts 1999, No. 220, § 2.

§ 117-87-603. Definition

    For purposes of this subchapter, the term "head of the nurse licensing board" shall mean the Executive Director of the Arkansas State Board of Nursing.

History:

    Acts 1999, No. 220, § 3.

§ 17-87-604. Effective Date

    (a) The effective date of this Compact shall be July 1, 2000.

    (b) Upon the effective date of this compact, the licensing board shall participate in an evaluation of the effectiveness and operability of the compact. Upon completion of the evaluation, a report shall be submitted to the Legislative Council for its review.

History:

    Acts 1999, No. 220, § 4.

SUBCHAPTER 7 –MEDICATION ASSISTIVE PERSONS

§ 17-87-701. Definitions

As used in this subchapter:

(1) "Board" means the Arkansas State Board of Nursing;

(2) "Designated facility" means a type of facility determined by the board as an environment in which medication assistive persons may serve in accordance with the requirements of this subchapter and regulations promulgated by the board;

(3) "Medication assistive person" means a person who is certified by the board to administer certain nonprescription and legend drugs in designated facilities; and

(4) "Supervision" means the active oversight of patient care services while on the premises of a designated facility in a manner defined by the board.

History:

Acts 2005, No. 1423, § 4.

§ 17-87-702. Certificate Required.

In order to safeguard life and health, any person serving or offering to serve as a medication assistive person shall:

(1) Submit evidence that he or she is qualified to so serve; and

(2) Be certified as provided in this subchapter.

History:

Acts 2005, No. 1423, § 4.

§ 17-87-703. Designated Facilities.

(a) The Arkansas State Board of Nursing shall designate the types of facilities that may use medication assistive persons.

(b) (1) Designated facilities may not be required to use medication assistive persons.

(2) However, if a designated facility elects to use medication assistive personnel, the facility shall notify the board in a manner prescribed by the board.

History:

Acts 2005, No. 1423, § 4.

§ 17-87-704. Qualifications

(a) In order to be certified as a medication assistive person, an applicant shall submit to the Arkansas State Board of Nursing written evidence, verified by oath, that the applicant:

(1) (A) Is currently listed in good standing on the state's certified nurse aide registry;

(B) Has maintained registration on the state's certified nurse aide registry continuously for a minimum of one (1) year;

(C) Has completed at least one (1) continuous year of full-time experience as a certified nurse aide in this state;

(D) Is currently employed at a designated facility;

(E) Has a high school diploma or the equivalent;

(F) Has successfully completed a literacy and reading comprehension screening process approved by the board;

(G) Has successfully completed a medication assistive person training course of not less than one hundred (100) hours approved by the board; and

(H) Has successfully passed an examination on subjects the board determines; or

(2) (A) Has completed a portion of a nursing education program equivalent to the medication assistive person training course; and

(B) Passed the medication aide examination.

(b) The board may issue a certification as a medication assistive person by endorsement to an applicant who has been licensed or certified as a medication assistive person under the laws of another state or territory, if:

(1) In the opinion of the board, the applicant meets the qualifications of medication assistive persons in this state; and

(2) The board recommends certification.

(c) Any person holding a certification as a medication assistive person shall have the right to use the title "medication assistive person" and the abbreviation "M.A.P.".

History:

Acts 2005, No. 1423, § 4; 2007, No. 206, § 1.

§ 17-87-705. Scope of Work

(a) (1) A medication assistive person may perform the delegated nursing function of medication administration and related tasks in accordance with rules promulgated by the Arkansas State Board of Nursing.

(2) A medication assistive person shall perform medication administration and related tasks only:

(A) At a designated facility; and

(B) Under the supervision of a licensed nurse.

(3) (A) Medication administration shall be limited to the administration of nonprescription and legend drugs ordered by an authorized prescriber by the following methods:

(i) Orally;

(ii) Topically;

(iii) Drops for eye, ear, or nose;

(iv) Vaginally;

(v) Rectally;

(vi) Transdermally; and

(vii) Via oral inhaler.

(B) Medication administration by a medication assistive person shall not include controlled substances.

(b) A medication assistive person shall not:

(1) Receive, have access to, or administer any controlled substance;

(2) Administer parenteral, enteral, or injectable medications;

(3) Administer any substances by nasogastric or gastrostomy tubes;

(4) Calculate drug dosages;

(5) Destroy medication;

(6) Receive orders, either in writing or verbally, for new or changed medications;

(7) Transcribe orders from the medical record;

(8) Order initial medications;

(9) Evaluate medication error reports;

(10) Perform treatments;

(11) Conduct patient assessments or evaluations; or

(12) Engage in patient teaching activities.

History: Acts 2005, No. 1423, § 4.

§ 17-87-706. Renewal of Certifications

(a) (1) The Arkansas State Board of Nursing shall prescribe the procedure for the cyclical renewal of medication assistive person certifications.

(2) In each case, the board shall mail a notification for renewal to the medication assistive person at least thirty (30) days before the expiration date of the certification.

(b) (1) Upon receipt of the renewal application and the fee, the board shall verify the accuracy of the application.

(2) (A) If the board finds the application to be accurate, the board shall issue a certificate of renewal to the applicant.

(B) As a condition of certification renewal, a medication assistive person shall be:

(i) Currently listed in good standing on the state's certified nurse aide registry; and

(ii) Required to satisfactorily complete at least eight (8) hours of continuing medication education course work as required by the board.

(c) The renewal shall render the holder of the certificate a legal provider of medication assistive person services for the period stated in the certificate of renewal.

(d) Any medication assistive person who allows his or her certification to lapse by failing to renew the certification as provided in this section may be reinstated by the board on:

(1) Payment of the renewal fee plus a penalty; and

(2) Submission of evidence that the person currently meets the requirements to serve as a medication assistive person.

(e) Any person providing services as a medication assistive person during the time his or her certification has lapsed shall be considered to be providing services illegally and shall be subject to the penalties provided for violations of this subchapter.

History:

Acts 2005, No. 1423, § 4.

§ 17-87-707. Disciplinary Actions

(a) The Arkansas State Board of Nursing shall have sole authority to deny, suspend, revoke, or limit any medication assistive person certificate issued by the board or applied for in accordance with the provisions of this subchapter or to otherwise discipline a certificate holder upon proof that the person:

(1) Has been found guilty of or pleads guilty or nolo contendere to:

(A) Fraud or deceit in procuring or attempting to procure a medication assistive person certificate;

(B) Providing services as a medication assistive person without a valid certificate; or

(C) Committing a crime of moral turpitude;

(2) Is unfit or incompetent by reason of negligence, habits, or other causes;

(3) Is habitually intemperate or is addicted to the use of habit-forming drugs;

(4) Is mentally incompetent;

(5) Is guilty of unprofessional conduct;

(6) Has had a license, certificate, or registration revoked or suspended;

(7) Has been placed on probation or under disciplinary order in any jurisdiction;

(8) Has voluntarily surrendered a license, certification, or registration and has not been reinstated in any jurisdiction; or

(9) Has willfully or repeatedly violated any of the provisions of this subchapter.

(b) The board shall refuse to issue or shall revoke the certificate of any person who would be disqualified from employment under the provisions of § 20-33-213.

(c) Proceedings under this section shall be conducted in accordance with the Arkansas Administrative Procedure Act, § 25-15-201 et seq.

History: Acts 2005, No. 1423, § 4, Act 2009, No. 762.

§ 17-87-708. Penalty

(a) (1) It shall be a misdemeanor for any person to:

    (A) Sell or fraudulently obtain or furnish any medication assistive person's certificate, renewal, or record or aid or abet in any such sale or fraud;

    (B) Serve as a medication assistive person under cover of any certificate or record illegally or fraudulently obtained or signed or issued unlawfully or under fraudulent representation;

    (C) Serve as a medication assistive person unless certified by the Arkansas State Board of Nursing;

    (D) Use in connection with his or her name any of the following titles, names, or initials if the user is not properly certified under this subchapter:

        (i) Medication assistive person;

        (ii) M.A.P.;

        (iii) Medication aide;

        (iv) Medication technician;

        (v) Medication assistant;

        (vi) Certified medication aide;

        (vii) C.M.A.;

        (viii) Medication assistant – Certified;

        (ix) MA – C; or

        (x) Any other name, title, or initials that would cause a reasonable person to believe the user is certified under this subchapter;

    (E) Serve as a medication assistive person during the time his or her certification is suspended;

    (F) Conduct an education program for the preparation of medication assistive persons unless the program has been approved by the board; or

(G) Otherwise violate any provisions of this subchapter.

(2) (A) A misdemeanor under subdivision (a)(1) of this section shall be punishable by a fine of not less than twenty-five dollars ($25.00) or more than five hundred dollars ($500).

(B) Each subsequent offense shall be punishable by a fine of not more than five hundred dollars ($500) or by imprisonment of not more than thirty (30) days, or by both a fine and imprisonment.

(b) (1) After providing notice and a hearing, the board may levy civil penalties in an amount not to exceed one thousand dollars ($1,000) against a person or entity for each violation of this subchapter or regulations promulgated under this subchapter.

(2) Each day of violation shall be a separate offense.

(c) Unless a penalty assessed under this section is paid within fifteen (15) calendar days following the date for an appeal from the order, the board may file suit in Pulaski County Circuit Court to obtain a judgment for the amount of penalty not paid.

(d) The penalties permitted in this section shall be in addition to other penalties that may be imposed by the board under this subchapter.

History:

Acts 2005, No. 1423, § 4; 2007, No. 206, § 2.

§ 17-87-709. Injunction

(a) The Pulaski County Circuit Court is vested with jurisdiction and power to enjoin the unlawful provision of medication assistive person services in any county of the State of Arkansas in a proceeding initiated by the Arkansas State Board of Nursing, any member of the board, or any citizen in this state.

(b) (1) The issuance of an injunction shall not relieve a person from criminal prosecution for violation of the provisions of this subchapter.

(2) The remedy of injunction is to be in addition to liability for criminal prosecution.

History:

Acts 2005, No. 1423, § 4.

§ 17-87-710. Medication Assistive Person Advisory Committee

(a) (1) The Medication Assistive Person Advisory Committee is created as an advisory committee to the Arkansas State Board of Nursing.

(2) The committee shall assist the board in implementing the provisions of this subchapter regarding medication assistive persons.

(b) The board shall appoint six (6) members to be approved by the Governor who have the following qualifications:

(1) Two (2) members shall be certified medication assistive persons;

(2) One (1) member shall be a licensed nursing home administrator who has worked in that capacity for at least five (5) years;

(3) One (1) member shall be a registered nurse who has been in a practice using certified nurse aides for at least five (5) years;

(4) One (1) member shall be a lay person representing the interest of consumers of health care services; and

(5) One (1) member shall be a nursing faculty member of an Arkansas nursing education program.

(c) Members shall serve three-year terms.

(d) The board may remove any committee member after notice and hearing for incapacity, incompetence, neglect of duty, or malfeasance in office.

(e) The members of the committee shall serve without compensation but may receive expense reimbursement in accordance with § 25-16-902.

History:

Acts 2005, No. 1423, § 4; 2007, No. 206, § 3.

§ 17-87-711.   Applicability of Subchapter

Nothing in this subchapter relieves a nurse from the responsibility of assessing each patient daily.

History:

Acts 2005, No. 1423, § 4.